Please return/renew this item by the last date
shown. Books may be renewed by
telephoning, writing to or calling in at any
library or on the Internet.

Northamptonshire Libraries and Information Service

**Northamptonshire
County Council**

www.northamptonshire.gov.uk/leisure/libraries/

Materials

KINGFISHER

Kingfisher Publications Plc
New Penderel House
283–288 High Holborn
London WC1V 7HZ
www.kingfisherpub.com

First published by Kingfisher Publications Plc 2005
2 4 6 8 10 9 7 5 3 1

1TR/0505/PROSP/RNB/140MA/F

Copyright © Kingfisher Publications Plc 2005

A CIP catalogue record for this book is available from the British Library.

ISBN–13: 978 0 7534 1110 0
ISBN–10: 0 7534 1110 5

Editor: Vicky Weber
Senior designer: Carol Ann Davis
Picture research manager: Cee Weston-Baker
DTP manager: Nicky Studdart
Production controller: Jessamy Oldfield

Printed in China

Acknowledgements
The publisher would like to thank the following for permission to reproduce their material. Every care has been taken to trace copyright holders. However, if there have been unintentional omissions or failure to trace copyright holders, we apologise and will, if informed, endeavour to make corrections in any future edition.
b = bottom, c = centre, l = left, t = top, r = right

Photographs: 1 Getty Imagebank; 2–3 Alamy/Creatas; 4–5 Alamy/Greg Wright; 6–7 Getty Taxi; 8bl Corbis; 9cl Getty Photodisc; 9tr Getty Imagebank; 9br Getty Imagebank; 10l Getty Rubberball; 10–11 Getty Stone; 11tr Getty Brand X; 12bl Science Photo Library/Colin Cuthbert; 12r Alamy/Denis Hallinan; 13t Getty Stone; 13b Alamy/Sally Greenhill; 14–15 Corbis/Ron Watts; 14b Corbis/Lester Lefkowitz; 15b Getty Imagebank; 16c Corbis/Gary Braasch; 16b Getty Imagebank; 17 Corbis/Thomas Hartwell; 18b Corbis/David Samuel Robbins; 19t Photonica; 19br Alamy/Panorama Stock; 20–21 Getty Imagebank; 20b Getty Lonely Planet; 21tl Getty Brand X; 21br Rex Features; 22b Corbis/James Marshall; 23t Getty Photodisc; 23b NASA; 24 Corbis/Joel W. Rogers; 25t Getty Imagebank; 25bl Getty Brand X; 26 Getty Stone; 27tl Alamy/Troy and Mary Parlee; 27br Rex Features; 28cr Getty Stone; 28bl Corbis/Owen Franken; 29tl Alamy; 29b Corbis/Charles O'Rear; 30c Corbis/David H. Seawell; 30–31b Corbis/Patrik Giardino; 31tr Corbis; 31br Alamy/D. Hurst; 32–33t Corbis/Richard Hamilton Smith; 32bl Getty Imagebank; 32br Corbis/Wolfgang Kaehler; 33l Getty Imagebank; 33br Corbis/Ariel Skelley; 34l Science Photo Library/Paul Whitehill; 34c Science Photo Library/Eye of Science; 35tl Corbis; 35b Corbis/Jim Cummins; 36bl Science Photo Library/Geoff Tompkinson; 37tl Corbis; 38 Getty Imagebank; 38b Corbis; 39tl Alamy/Dex Image; 39 Corbis/Ariel Skelley; 40b Getty Imagebank; 40r Getty Imagebank; 41tl Alamy/James Frank; 41r Getty Imagebank; 48 Alamy/Tim Brightmore

Project co-ordinator: Carron Brown
Commissioned photography on pages 42–47 by Andy Crawford
Thank you to models Hayley Sapsford, Cameron Green and Joley Theodoulou

KFYK Kingfisher Young Knowledge

Materials

Clive Gifford

Contents

What are materials? 6

Liquids and solids 8

Floating and sinking 10

Stretchy and bendy 12

Rocky world 14

Building blocks 16

Clay and ceramics 18

Using glass 20

Mighty metals 22

Mixing metals 24

Wonderful wood 26

28 Working with wood

30 The purpose of paper

32 Natural fabrics

34 Man-made fabrics

36 Making plastics

38 Plastics around us

40 Ready to recycle

42 Project

44 Project

46 Project

48 Index

What are materials?

Materials are all around us. They are the objects that make up the world we live in. Some materials, such as rocks, are natural. Others, for example, plastic and glass, are made by people.

Using materials

People use materials all the time. This picture shows many different sorts. There are liquid paints, plastic paint bottles and rollers, which are all man-made. There are also wooden shelves and a table, paper and cotton clothing. These are natural materials.

man-made – *made by people*

Liquids and solids

Liquids are wet and can flow easily. Solid materials cannot flow, and have a definite shape. Heat turns some solids into liquids.

Shaping shoes
Solid iron is heated to make it soft and easy to shape into a horseshoe.

Liquid gold
When gold is heated, it becomes a red, hot liquid, which can be poured and shaped.

flow – *run like water*

Hot chocolate ice

Ice-cream can be dipped into warm, melted chocolate. Once cool, the chocolate goes hard, and becomes a tasty treat.

Candlelight

A hot flame melts wax, which then runs down a candle. When the wax cools, it solidifies.

Melting lolly

In warm weather, you have to eat an ice-lolly quickly before it melts. This is because the solid ice becomes watery when the sun warms it.

solidifies – turns from liquid to solid

Floating and sinking

Some materials are very light and can float on water or even in the air. Other materials, such as rock, are much heavier and normally sink.

Up, up and away

Helium is a gas that is lighter than air. Balloons can be filled with helium to make them float in the air.

air – *the mixture of gases we breathe*

Sinking like a stone

Many materials, such as stones, are too heavy to float in water. This means they just sink to the bottom if they are thrown into a river or sea.

Floating fun

Both this raft and the children's lifejackets are made of rubber. They float on water when filled with air. This means they are great to play with in the sea – and keep you safe too!

gas – *a shapeless substance, such as air, that is not solid or liquid*

Stretchy and bendy

If you stretch or bend some materials, they return to their normal shape once you let go. Other materials stay in the shape you pull them.

Boing! Boing!

A spring is made of coiled wire. It jumps back to its usual shape after it has been squashed or pulled. That is why a pogo stick lets you bounce up and down.

flexible – bendy, stretchy

High flyer

Vaulting poles are very flexible and can bend a long way. They help athletes fly high up into the air.

Stretchy hairbands

Hairbands are often made of elastic. They stretch as they tie up long hair. Then they return to their normal shape and keep a perfect ponytail in place.

elastic – stretchy material

Rocky world

Rocks make up the earth's crust. They are ancient materials and some are more than 4 billion years old. Rocks such as chalk are crumbly and soft, while others, like granite, are hard and tough.

Hot rocks

Burning hot lava comes from inside the earth. It is runny rock, which turns hard as it cools.

the earth's crust – the surface of the planet where we live

Layer upon layer

Some rocks lie in layers, called strata. Over millions of years, the layers can become bent, just like the sandstone in the picture.

Wear and tear

Cold, heat, water and wind all wear away rocks little by little. Over time, amazing shapes, such as these arches, can form.

arches – *curved openings in rock*

Building blocks

Rock is a very useful material that is strong, tough and hard-wearing. It can be crushed up or used in big chunks to make, for example, buildings, roads and statues.

Mining for marble

Rock is mined in a quarry. Here, marble is being dug up. Marble is a hard rock that can be polished and used for floors and statues.

Big chunks

For centuries, rocks have been used to build walls. Giant blocks make up this old wall in Peru – they must have been very difficult to put in place.

mined – *dug out of the ground*

Sparkling jewels

All rocks are made from minerals. Some minerals form beautiful and precious gemstones, such as these rubies and diamonds.

Living in the past

Rocks can be carved into sculptures which last a very long time. The Great Sphinx in Egypt was shaped from limestone rock around 4,500 years ago.

minerals – *natural substances in the earth's surface that make rocks*

Clay and ceramics

Clay and ceramics are soft, earthy materials that are dug out of the ground. They can be shaped easily. When they are heated, they dry out and become very hard.

Round and round

Clay can be shaped on a potter's wheel, like the one below. Some clay objects dry out and harden in the sun. Others have to be fired in a hot oven called a kiln.

fired – *baked at a very high temperature*

Perfect pools
Clay and ceramics are used to make tiles and bricks. Tiles form a smooth, waterproof surface that is perfect for lining swimming pools.

Pretty paints
Clay objects can be painted brightly. A liquid called a glaze is often brushed on. This makes the clay waterproof.

Using glass

Glass is made mainly from sand heated to a high temperature. While hot, glass can be shaped. For example, it can be pressed into window panes or blown into bottles.

Playing marbles

Some glass is very thin and breaks easily. Thick glass is strong and great for making toy marbles.

Sealed in jars

Many foods containing liquids, such as pickles, are kept in glass jars because they are waterproof and airtight. The food is stored for years without going off.

airtight – closed to the air

Glass of milk

Glass can be coloured or clear (see-through). A lot of drinking glasses are clear, so that you can keep an eye on what you are drinking.

With a huff and a puff

Glass objects can be made by glass-blowing. A blob of runny glass is put on the end of a tube. Blowing into the tube inflates the glass like a balloon. When the glass cools, it sets hard.

inflates – *fills with gas*

Mighty metals

Metals are shiny materials found in rocks in the ground. Some metals are hard and tough. Others are softer and weak. As they can be cut and bent, metals are used to make many different things.

Feeling the heat

Cooking pans are often made from metals such as copper. Heat can go straight through the metal to cook the food.

hed ih

valuable – worth a lot

Glittering gold

Precious metals, such as gold, are valuable to people. They can be made into jewellery or shaped into bars, called ingots, that are worth a lot of money.

Travelling light

In 2004, two robots landed on the planet Mars. Parts of the robots were made from lightweight metals. This made the journey to Mars easier.

lightweight – *not weighing very much*

Mixing metals

Two or more metals, or a metal and a non-metal, can be mixed together to form new materials called alloys. These alloys are useful as they can be light, strong and very hard-wearing.

Space Needle

The Space Needle towers over the American city of Seattle. It is made from steel, the world's most common alloy. Steel is used to make many things, from cutlery to cars.

cutlery – knives, forks and spoons

Not worth its weight in gold

In the past, coins were made from precious metals such as silver and gold. Now, they are made from much cheaper metals, often alloys.

Bold as brass

Brass is made from mixing the metals zinc and copper. It is tough and hard, but can still be shaped easily. Many musical instruments are made from brass.

Wonderful wood

Wood is a useful natural material. It comes from trees. Each type of tree is made of a different kind of wood – some are soft and others are tough.

Collecting wood

Forest workers use cutting machines, called chainsaws, to chop down trees. The trees are then cut up into logs.

logs – *cut-up parts of a tree*

To the sawmill

Logs are carried by trucks or floated down rivers. They are taken to a place called a sawmill. There, different sizes and thicknesses of wood are cut and prepared for use.

Soft landing

Leftover pieces of wood can be cut up into wooden chips. These are very soft, so they are often used on the floors of playgrounds.

Working with wood

Woodwork has been an important trade and a popular hobby for thousands of years. Today, wood is used to make many objects, including buildings, boats and furniture.

Finely shaped

It is easy to cut and shape wood using tools. This person is working on a piece of wood with a metal tool called a chisel.

Family fun

Nearly all wood floats on water. This means it is really good for making rafts, boats and ships.

trade – job, business

Woody pencils

Coloured pencils are made from a long stick of colour covered with a painted wooden case. Cedar wood is often used to make pencils, because it is strong.

Bright beach huts

These wooden beach huts are brightly painted. The paint helps protect the wood from rain. If wood stays wet for a long time, it starts to go bad and can fall apart.

The purpose of paper

Paper is a thin, lightweight material. It can be bent and folded easily. There are a lot of different uses for paper. Most often it is used for writing or printing on.

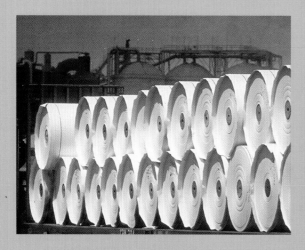

Making paper

Most paper is made in rolls in factories. It is usually produced from tiny bits of wood, but it can also be made from old paper or from rags.

produced – made

Writing on paper

There are many types of writing paper. Notepaper is thin; formal writing paper is thick; and greeting cards are stiff and stand up tall. All are smooth to write on.

Daily paper

Newsprint is a special type of paper used for newspapers. It is made from ground-up wood, and is thin and cheap to produce.

Paper containers

Milk and juice cartons are made from paper. They are covered in plastic to make them waterproof. Many other papers, such as kitchen towels, soak up liquids.

formal – *proper, official*

Natural fabrics

Fabrics are made from long strands of material, called threads, that are woven together. Many threads come from plants and animals.

girls wearing kimonos

Smooth as silk

Silk is a beautiful fabric. It comes from thread spun by a silkworm while it is in its cocoon. It takes 3,000 cocoons to make a kimono.

silkworm – *a type of caterpillar*

Cotton buds

Cotton is a plant with big, fluffy buds, called bolls. These are collected from the fields, and washed. They are then pulled into long threads and spun into fabric.

Warm wool

Wool comes from the coats of sheep and other animals, such as some goats and camels. It can be knitted into snug clothes and blankets.

cocoon – a covering around an insect made from silky thread

Man-made fabrics

Some fabrics are not natural, but can be made from a natural raw material, such as coal. They are man-made, and are called synthetic fabrics.

Velcro hooks and loops
Velcro is made from one strip of small hooks and another strip of tiny loops. The hooks catch in the loops when the strips are pressed together.

raw material – material used to make other materials

Flying high

Nylon is a light, strong fabric. It is used not just for clothing, but also for ropes, fishing nets and even parachutes.

Synthetics in sport

Synthetic fabrics are often used to make sports clothing. This boy's shorts, vest and trainers are all made from different lightweight fabrics.

Making plastics

Plastics are always man-made. People have learned to make them out of other substances, especially oil.

Plastic penguins

When heated, plastic can be shaped easily. It can be stretched and made into tubes or sheets. Or it can be poured into moulds to make objects such as these toy penguins.

Creating cartons

To make a bottle, hot plastic is poured into a mould. A machine blows in air, which presses the plastic to the sides of the mould. The cool plastic sets in a bottle shape.

oil – a greasy liquid

Fabulous for food

Polystyrene is plastic foam. The foam is made by blowing bubbles of air into hot plastic. It keeps things warm and is lightweight – perfect for holding food.

moulds – *hollow, shaped containers*

Plastics around us

Plastic is used to make all sorts of objects, from furniture to paints and toys. Plastic does not rot quickly. This causes a problem with rubbish. Re-using and recycling plastic helps cut down waste (see page 40).

Fine brickwork
Plastic bricks are hard-wearing, tough and easy to clean. Many plastics are also cheap to make.

Beach life

Plastics can be made very light in weight. Beachballs, balloons and blow-up swimming pools are all made of plastic that can be filled up with air.

Singing in the rain

Plastic sheets can be cut and glued or sewn together to make brightly coloured, waterproof clothes. This makes plastic an ideal material for raincoats, hats and wellies.

rot – *go bad, go off*

Ready to recycle

Many unwanted materials can be collected and turned into new materials. This is called recycling. Recycling helps cut down waste.

the recycling symbol

Recycling at home

Many materials can be recycled, for example, glass, plastic and paper. This family is sorting out its recycling rubbish. Each material goes in a different container.

Fizzy drinks to fleeces

A lot of fleece jackets are made from old fizzy drink bottles. The plastic bottles are shredded and turned into thread. About 25 bottles are needed for a fleece.

Swinging time

Some items are re-used rather than recycled. This old tyre, for example, has been given a new job as a great swing.

shredded – *cut up into very small pieces*

Boat slalom

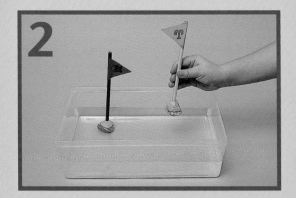

Blow a boat around a course

See how one material floats and another sinks with this fun and easy project.

You will need
- Waterproof modelling dough
- Two stones
- Two pencils
- Two pieces of card, 3cm x 3cm x 2cm, decorated with your motif
- Glue
- Wide, shallow container
- Water
- Scissors
- Plastic cup
- Drinking straw 10cm long
- Square piece of coloured-in paper, 6cm x 6cm

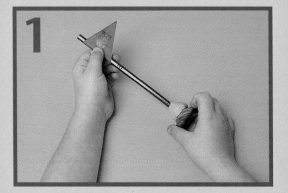

1 Press modelling dough onto a stone and push a pencil into the top of it. Glue the card onto the end of the pencil as a flag. Now you have a slalom pole. Repeat.

2 Half fill the container with water and place the slalom poles in the middle of the bowl, with 10cm between each. The poles should stick out of the water.

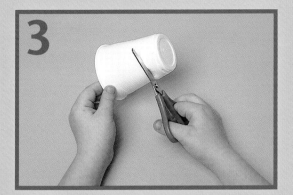

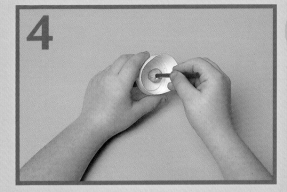

To make a boat, cut around a plastic cup, about 2.5cm from its bottom. Stick modelling dough into the base.

For the mast, push a plastic straw into the modelling dough so that it sticks straight up in the middle of the base of the cup.

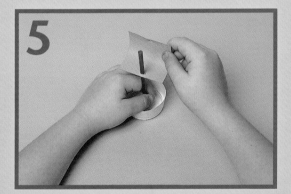

Put your boat at the start of the slalom course and blow it around the poles. Take it in turns with a friend to send your boat whizzing around the course.

With scissors, make a small hole in the top and bottom of the paper. Push the paper onto the straw through the holes. You have a sailboat that will float!

Balloon head

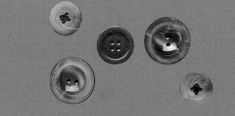

Papier mâché model

See how you can use lots of materials to create a sculpture of a head.

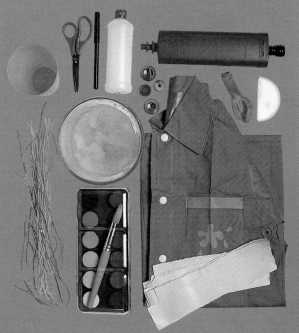

You will need
- Newspaper
- Overall (optional)
- Balloon
- Balloon pump (optional)
- Wide-necked mug or vase
- Strips of thin paper
- Colour paints
- Paint brushes
- Bowl of ready-mixed wallpaper paste
- Glue
- Coloured buttons
- Wool or silvery strands
- Thick pen

1

Cover the work surface with newspaper. Blow up the balloon. Place the knotted end of the balloon in the mug or vase.

2

Take a strip of paper, cover it in paste and stick it on the balloon. Continue doing this until the balloon is covered. Leave to dry.

3

Repeat step 2 three more times, so that your balloon is covered in four layers of paper strips. Let the head dry fully for a day.

4

Now paint your balloon head in a skin colour – brown, pink or white. Make sure the whole head is covered. Let the paint dry.

5

Decorate the papier mâché balloon with wool or silvery strands for the hair, and buttons for the eyes and nose. Colour in a mouth in pen. You could use other materials, such as paper hair, for more model heads.

Chocolate crispies

A tasty chocolate treat
See how chocolate can change from a solid into a liquid, and back into a solid again.

microwave not shown

You will need
- Microwave
- Microwavable bowl
- 1 large bar (150g) of cooking chocolate
- Large spoon
- 70g rice crispies
- Small spoon
- Set of cake cases
- Plate
- Airtight container

1 Break up the bar of chocolate into single pieces and put them in the bowl. Microwave this for 90 seconds on full power.

2 Ask an adult to take the bowl out of the microwave, and stir the chocolate. If it has not all melted, heat it for another 15 seconds.

Be careful! Heated chocolate can burn you. Ask an adult to help.

Sprinkle the rice crispies on the melted chocolate. Stir the mixture until all the crispies are coated and the chocolate is used up.

Spoon a dollop of mixture into each cake case and put on a plate to cool for an hour. Use up all of the mixture.

Once cooled and hardened, the chocolate crispies are ready to be stored in an airtight container...

...or eaten immediately!

Index

air 10, 11, 37
alloys 24–25
bending 12–13
building 16, 17, 28
cartons 31, 36
ceramics 18–19
chocolate 9, 46, 47
clay 18–19
clothes 6, 32, 33, 35, 39, 40
coal 34
coins 25
cold 9, 15, 21, 36, 47
cotton 6, 33
elastic 13
fabrics 32–33, 34–35
floating 10–11, 42
gases 10, 11, 21
gemstones 17
glass 6, 20–21, 40
heat 8, 9, 15, 18, 20, 22, 36, 37
helium 10

jewellery 16, 17, 23
lava 14
liquids 6, 8–9, 20, 31, 46
metals 22–23, 24, 25, 28
mining 16
musical instruments 25
oil 36
paper 6, 30–31, 40
plastic 6, 31, 36–37, 38–39, 40, 41
polystyrene 37
recycling 38, 40–41
rocks 6, 10, 14–15, 16–17, 22
rubber 10, 11
sand 20
silk 32
sinking 10–11, 42
solids 8–9, 46
stretching 12–13
water 11, 15, 42
wood 6, 26–27, 28–29, 30,
wool 33